Hussein Osman

Time Series Prediction Using Neural network

Hussein Osman

Time Series Prediction Using Neural network

LAP LAMBERT Academic Publishing

Imprint

Any brand names and product names mentioned in this book are subject to trademark, brand or patent protection and are trademarks or registered trademarks of their respective holders. The use of brand names, product names, common names, trade names, product descriptions etc. even without a particular marking in this work is in no way to be construed to mean that such names may be regarded as unrestricted in respect of trademark and brand protection legislation and could thus be used by anyone.

Cover image: www.ingimage.com

Publisher:
LAP LAMBERT Academic Publishing
is a trademark of
International Book Market Service Ltd., member of OmniScriptum Publishing Group
17 Meldrum Street, Beau Bassin 71504, Mauritius

Printed at: see last page
ISBN: 978-613-9-45966-7

Copyright © Hussein Osman
Copyright © 2019 International Book Market Service Ltd., member of OmniScriptum Publishing Group

Time Series Prediction Using Neural Networks

By

Hussein Abdulatif Hussein Osman

DEDICATION

To my family and all who supported me in my studies.

To every seeker of knowledge.

I dedicate this research.

AKNOWLEDGEMENTS

I would like to express my sincere gratitude to my supervisor **Dr. Ahmed Abdallah Mohamed Imam**, for his interest, help and invaluable guidance given throughout the work for this project.

Further, I would like to thank all my friends for providing valuable information by answering my inquiries.

ABSTRACT

Neural networks are an artificial intelligence tool for modeling of complex functions. During the last decade they have been widely applied to the domain of time series prediction and their importance in this field is growing. The aim of this work is to explore the potential of the Artificial Neural Network in the field of time series prediction problems, emphasizing the issues particularly important with respect to the neural network approach to this task.

The problem of time series prediction is formulated as a system identification problem, where the input to the system is the past values of a time series, and its desired output is the future values of a time series. Auto regressive neural network model (ARx NN) is designed and optimized using error back propagation algorithm.

Three cases are considered and simulated. The obtained results showed acceptable prediction error.

TABLE OF CONTENTS

Dedication	i
Acknowledgement	ii
Abstract	iii
Table of contents	iv
CHAPTER 1 INTRODUCTION	**1**
1.1 Overview	1
1.1.1 Basic definitions	3
1.1.1.1 Learning algorithms	4
1.1.1.1.1 Supervised learning	4
1.1.1.1.2 Unsupervised learning	5
1.1.1.2 Time series signal	5
1.2 Problem definition	7
1.3 Dissertation aims and objectives	7
1.4 Methodology	8
1.3 Dissertation organization	8
CHAPTER 2 MODELS AND LEARNING OF NEURAL SYSTEMS	**10**
2.1 Introduction	10
2.2 Models of artificial neural networks	10
2.2.1 Feedforward network	10
2.2.2 Feedback network	13

2.3	Neural processing		15
2.4	Learning and adaptation		18
2.5	Neural network learning rules		19
	2.5.1	Hebbian learning rule	20
	2.5.2	Perceptron learning rule	21
	2.5.3	Delta learning rule	22
	2.5.4	Widrow-Hoff learning rule	23
	2.5.5	Correlation learning rule	24
	2.5.6	Winner-take-all learning rule	24
	2.5.7	Outstar learning rule	25
2.6	Summary		26

CHAPTER 3   TIME SERIES PROCESSING
USING NEURAL NETWORKS   27

3.1	Introduction	27
3.2	Multi-layer feedforward	27
	3.2.1 Error back-propagation training	28
	3.2.2 Learning factors	33
	3.2.2.1 Initial weights	34
	3.2.2.2 Cumulative weight adjustment versus incremental updating	34
	3.2.2.3 Steepness of the activation function	35
	3.2.2.4 Learning constant	36
3.3	Time-delay neural network	37
3.4	Jordan network	38
3.5	Elman network	39

3.6	Multi-recurrent network	39
3.7	Other network architectures	41
3.8	Summary	42

CHAPTER 4   DESIGN OF ANN IN TIME SERIES   43

4.1	Introduction	43
4.2	Variable selection	43
4.3	Data collection	43
4.4	Data preprocessing	44
4.5	Data Partitioning	46
4.6	Neural network design	48
	4.6.1 Number of hidden neurons	48
	4.6.2 Number of output neurons	50
	4.6.3 Transfer functions	51
4.7	Evaluation of the system	51
4.8	Training the ANN	52
4.9	Implementation	52
4.10	Summary	53

CHAPTER 5   SIMULATION RESULTS   54

5.1	Introduction	54
5.2	Case study 1: Sinusoid plus simulated Gaussian white noise	54
5.3	Case study 2: River Nile basin	60
5.4	Case study 3: Sunspot	63
5.6	Summary	65

CHAPTER 6 CONCLUSIONS AND
            FURTHER WORK   **66**

6.1   Conclusions   **66**
6.2   Further work   **68**

REFERENCES   **69**

CHAPTER 1

INTRODUCTION

1.1 OVERVIEW

A *neural network* is a massively parallel distributed processor that has a natural propensity for storing experiential knowledge and making it available for use. It resembles the brain in two respects [1]:

    1. Knowledge is acquired by the network through a learning process.

    2. Interconnection strengths known as synaptic weights are used to store the knowledge.

The study of artificial neural networks (ANNs) has been inspired in part by the observation that biological learning systems are built of very complex webs of interconnected neurons. In rough analogy, artificial neural networks are built out of a densely interconnected set of simple units, where each unit takes a number of real-valued inputs (possibly the outputs of other units) and produces a single real-valued output, which may become input to other units [2].

To develop a feel for this analogy, let us consider a few facts from neurobiology. The human brain, for example, is estimated to contain a densely interconnected network of approximately 10^{11} neurons, each connected, on average, to 10^4 others. Neuron activity is typically excited or inhibited through connections to other neurons. The fastest neuron switching times are known to be on the order of 10^{-3} seconds, quite slow compared to computer switching speeds of 10^{-10} seconds. Yet humans are able to make surprisingly complex decisions, surprisingly quickly. For example, it requires approximately 10^{-1} seconds to visually recognize one's mother. Notice the sequence of neuron firings that can take place during this 10^{-1}-second interval cannot possibly be longer than a few hundred steps, given that the information-processing abilities of biological neural systems must follow from highly parallel processes operating on representations that are distributed over many neurons. One motivation for ANN systems is to capture this kind of highly parallel computation based on distributed representations. Most ANN software runs on sequential machines emulating distributed processes, although faster versions of the algorithms have also been implemented on highly parallel machines and on specialized hardware designed specifically for ANN applications [2].

While ANNs are loosely motivated by biological neural systems, there are many complexities to biological neural systems that are not modeled by ANNs, and many features of ANNs are known to be inconsistent with biological systems [2]. The ANN related research can be divided into two directions:

1. research targeting at exploring the properties of biological systems by means of neural networks (computational neuroscience) and

2. research targeting on development of systems capable to approximate complex functions efficiently and independent of whether they "mirror" biological ones or not.

1.1.1 BASIC DEFINITIONS

The structure of a neural network of most commonly used type is schematically shown in Figure 1.1. It consists of several layers of processing units (also termed neurons, nodes).

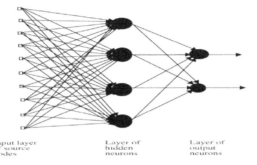

Figure 1.1: Basic structure of a multi-layer perceptron

The input values (input data) are fed to the neurons in the so-called *input layer* in the left part of Figure 1.1. The input values are processed (the data processing in the neurons is discussed later in this chapter) within the individual neurons of the input layer and then the output values of these neurons are forwarded to the neurons in the *hidden layer*. The arrows indicate connections from the input nodes to hidden nodes, along which the output values of the input nodes are passed on to the hidden nodes. These values obtained as inputs by the hidden nodes are again processed within them and passed on to either the output layer or to the next hidden layer (there can be more than one hidden layer). Each connection has an associated parameter indicating the strength of this connection, the so-called *weight*. By changing the weights in a specific manner, the network can" learn" to map patterns presented at the input layer to target values on the output layer. The description of the procedure, by means of which this weight adaptation is performed, is called *learning* or *training algorithm*.

1.1.1.1 LEARNING ALGORITHMS

Contrary to such a simple case as the OR function is, usually the weights of the ANN must be adjusted using some learning algorithm in order for the ANN to be able to approximate the target function with a sufficient precision. To find the optimal neural network structure for a solution to a particular problem, training algorithms have to be used.

The type of learning is determined by the manner in which the parameter changes take place. In a general sense, the learning process may be classified as follows [1]:

1. Learning with a teacher, also referred to as supervised learning.
2. Learning without a teacher, also referred to as unsupervised Learning.

1.1.1.1.1 SUPERVISED LEARNING

This form of learning assumes the availability of a labeled (i.e., ground-truthed) set of training data made up of N input-output examples:

$$T = \{(x_i, d_i)\}_{i=1}^{N} \quad (1.1)$$

where $\mathbf{x}_i$ = input vector of ith example.

d_i = desired (target) response of ith example, assumed to be scalar for convenience of presentation.

N = sample size.

Given the training sample T, the requirement is to compute the free parameters of the neural network so that the actual output y_i of the neural network due to $\mathbf{x}_i$ is close enough to d_i for all i in a statistical sense. For example, we may use the mean-square error

$$E(n) = \frac{1}{N}\sum_{i=1}^{N}(d_i - y_i)^2 \qquad (1.2)$$

as the index of performance to be minimized.

1.1.1.1.2 UNSUPERVISED LEARNING

Turning next to unsupervised learning, adjustment of synaptic weights may be carried through the use of neurobiological principles such as Hebbian learning and competitive learning [1].

1.1.1.2 TIME SERIES SIGNAL

A time series is a set of observations x_t, each one being recorded at a specific time t. A discrete time series is one where the set of times at which observations are made is a discrete set. Continuous time series are obtained by recording observations continuously over some time interval. An example of a discrete time series can be seen in Figure 1.2.

Analyzing time series data led to the decomposition of time series into components. Each component is defined to be a major factor or force that can affect any time series. Three major components of time series have been identified. *Trend* refers to the long-term tendency of a time series to rise or fall. *Seasonality* refers to the periodic behavior of a time series within a specified period of time. The fluctuation in a time series after the trend and seasonal components have been removed is termed as the *irregular* component.

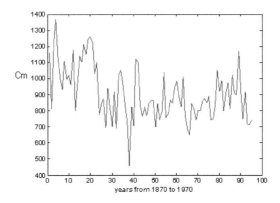

Figure 1.2: Annual River Nile flow

If a time series can be exactly predicted from past knowledge, it is termed as *deterministic*. Otherwise it is termed as *statistical*, where past knowledge can only indicate the probabilistic structure of future behavior. A statistical series can be considered as a single realization of some *stochastic process*. A stochastic process is a family of random variables defined on a probability space. A realization of a stochastic process is a sample path of this process.

1.2 PROBLEM DEFINITION

Most of Natural phenomena are characterized by stochastic and nonlinear behavior, so, it is hard to model and predict their future behavior using deterministic models.

1.3 DISSERTATION AIMS AND OBJECTIVES

The aim of this work is to explore the potential of the Artificial Neural Network in the field of time series prediction problem, emphasizing the issues particularly important with respect to the neural network approach to this task.

Polynomial neural networks [3] are feedforward networks that use higher order correlations of their input components. This makes them attractive for use in system identification and modeling since they can perform non-linear mappings with only a single layer of units.

Polynomial neural networks [3] architectures structured will be applied to the time series prediction problem. Traditional approaches to prediction were based either on finding a law underlying the given dynamic process or phenomenon or on discovering some strong empirical regularities in the observation of the time series. For the first case, if a law can be discovered and analytically described, e.g. by a set of differential equations, then by solving them we can predict the future if the initial conditions are completely known and satisfied. The problem with this approach is that usually information about dynamic processes is only partial and incomplete.

In the second case, if there is a time series consisting of samples of a periodic process, it can be modeled by the superposition of sinusoids generated by a set of second order differential equations. In real-world problems though, regularities such as periodicity are masked by noise and some phenomena are described by chaotic time series in which the data seem random without apparent periodicities [3].

1.4 METHODOLOGY

Multilayer Perceptron NNs are used to address the time series prediction problem. Error Backpropagation algorithm is used for the training.

NeuroShell2. package is used for the design and simulation of the cases considered in this work. NeuroShell 2 is a software program that mimics the human brain's ability to classify patterns or to make predictions or decisions based upon past experience. The human brain relies on neural stimuli while the neural network uses data sets.

NeuroShell 2 enables us to build sophisticated custom problem solving applications without programming. We tell the network what we are trying to predict or classify, and NeuroShell 2 will be able to "learn" patterns from training data and be able to make its own classifications, predictions, or decisions when presented with new data.

1.4 DISSERTATION ORGANIZATION

Chapter 2 deals with the models and learning of neural networks. It covers the topics of feedforward and feedback neural networks, and seven basic learning rules using supervised or unsupervised mode. An overview of neural network processing is also given.

Chapter 3 gives the processing of time series signals using neural network is formulated, multi-layer feedforward network is also formulated, and error back-propagation learning algorithm is presented. Some common other neural networks architecture are also summarized.

Chapter 4 gives the steps of designing an artificial neural network for time series prediction.

Chapter 5 gives results of the simulations of three case studies conducted on different time series.

Chapter 6 gives the conclusions of this dissertation and recommendations for further work in this area of research.

CHAPTER 2

MODELS AND LEARNING OF NEURAL SYSTEMS

2.1 INTRODUCTION

Artificial neural networks can be defined as physical cellular networks that are able to acquire, store, and utilize experiential knowledge. This definition has been related to the network's capabilities and performance [4]. At this point, knowing the definition of the artificial neural network neuron model, we may benefit from another definition. The neural network can also be defined as an *interconnection of neurons, such that neuron outputs are connected, through weights, to all other neurons including themselves; both lag-free and delay connection are allowed.*

2.2 MODELS OF ARTIFICIAL NEURAL NETWORKS
2.2.1 FEEDFORWARD NETWORK

If we consider an elementary *feed forward architecture* of m neurons receiving n inputs as shown in Figure 2.1(a). Its output and input vectors are, respectively

$$\mathbf{o} = [\ o_1\ o_2\ ...\ o_m\ ]^T \qquad (2.1)$$

$$\mathbf{x} = [\ x_1\ x_2\ ...\ x_n\ ]^T \qquad (2.2)$$

Weight w_{ij} connects the i'th neuron with the jth input. We thus can write the activation value for the i'th neuron as

$$net_i = \sum_{j=1}^{n} w_{ij} x_j \quad \text{for } i = 1, 2, ..., m \qquad (2.3)$$

The following nonlinear transformation [Equation (2.4)] involving the activation function $f(net_i)$, for $i = 1, 2, \ldots, m$, completes the processing of **x**. The transformation, performed by each of the m neurons in the network, is a strongly nonlinear mapping expressed as

$$o_i = f(w_i^T x), \quad \text{for } i = 1, 2, \ldots, m \tag{2.4}$$

where weight vector w_i contains weights leading toward the i'th output node and is defined as follows

$$w_i = [\, w_{i1} \; w_{i2} \; \ldots \; w_{in} \,]^T \tag{2.5}$$

Introducing the nonlinear matrix operator Γ, the mapping of input space x to output space o implemented by the network can be expressed as follows

$$o = \Gamma[Wx] \tag{2.6}$$

where W is the *weight matrix,* also called the connection matrix.

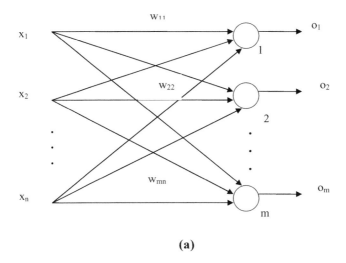

(a)

Chapter 2   Models and learning of neural systems

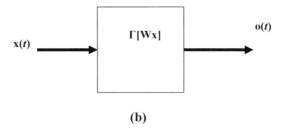

(b)

Figure 2.1: Single feedforward network: (a) interconnection scheme and (b) block diagram

The input and output vectors **x** and **o** are often called *input* and *output pattern*, respectively [4]. The mapping of an input pattern into an output pattern as shown in (2.6) is of the feedforward and instantaneous type, since it involves no time delay between the input **x**, and the output **o**. Thus we can write (2.6) in the explicit form involving time *t* as

$$o(t) = \Gamma[Wx(t)] \qquad (2.7)$$

Figure 2.1(b) shows the block diagram of the feedforward network. As can be seen, the generic feedforward network is characterized by the lack of feedback. This type of network can be connected in cascade to create a multilayer network. In such a network, the output of a layer is the input of the following layer. Even though the feedforward network has no explicit feedback connection when x(t) is mapped into o(t), the output values are often compared with "teacher's" information, which provides the desired output value, and also error signal can be employed for adapting the network's weights.

2.2.2 FEEDBACK NETWORK

A feedback network can be obtained from the feedforward network shown in Figure 2.1(a) by connecting the neuron's outputs to their inputs. The result is depicted in Figure 2.2(a). The essence of closing the feedback loop is to enable control of output o_i through outputs o_j, for $j = 1, 2, ..., m$. Such control is especially meaningful if the present output, say $o(t)$, controls the output at the following instance, $o(t + \Delta)$. The time Δ elapsed between t and $t + \Delta$ is introduced by the delay elements in the feedback loop as shown in Figure 2.2(a). Here the time delay Δ has a symbolic meaning; it is an analogy to the refractory period of an elementary biological neuron model. Using the notation introduced for feedforward networks, the mapping of $o(t + \Delta)$ can now be written as

$$o(t + \Delta) = \Gamma[Wo(t)] \tag{2.8}$$

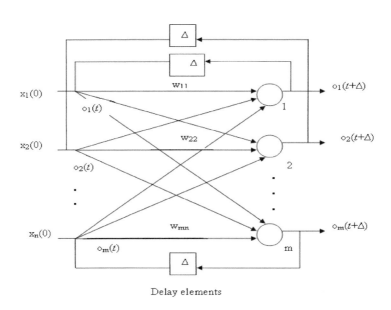

(a)

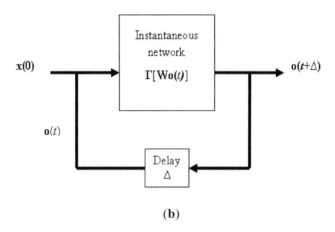

(b)

Figure2.2: Single layer discrete-time feedback network (a) interconnection scheme and (b) block diagram

Formula (2.8) is represented by the block diagram shown in Figure 2.2(b). Note that the input x(t) is only needed to initialize this network so that o(0) = x(0). The input is then removed and the system remains autonomous for t > 0. We thus consider her especial case of this feedback configuration, such that x(t) = x(0) and no input is provided to the network thereafter, or for t > 0 [4].

There are two main categories of single-layer feedback networks. If we consider time as a discrete variable and decide to observe the network performance at discrete time instants Δ, 2Δ, 3Δ, …, the system is called *discrete-time*. For notational convenience, the time step in discrete time networks is equated to unity, and the time instances are indexed by positive integers. Symbol Δ thus has the meaning of unity delay. For a discrete-time artificial neural system, we have converted (2.8) to the form

$$\mathbf{o}^{k+1} = \Gamma[\mathbf{Wo}^k], \quad \text{for } k = 1, 2, \ldots \tag{2.9}$$

where k is the instant number. The network in Figure 2.2 is called *recurrent* since its response at the $k + 1^{\text{th}}$ instant depends on the entire history of the network starting at $(k + 0)$. Indeed, we have from (2.9) a serial of nested solutions as follows:

$$\mathbf{o}^1 = \Gamma[\mathbf{Wx}^0]$$
$$\mathbf{o}^2 = \Gamma[\mathbf{W}\Gamma[\mathbf{Wx}^0]]$$
$$\ldots \tag{2.10}$$
$$\mathbf{o}^{k+1} = \Gamma[\mathbf{W}\Gamma[\ldots\Gamma[\mathbf{Wx}^0]\ldots]]$$

Recurrent networks typically operate with a discrete representation of data; they employ neurons with hard-limiting activation function. A system with discrete-time input and a discrete data representation is called an *automation*.

Equations (2.10) describe what we call the state $\mathbf{o}^k$ of the network at instants $k = 1, 2, \ldots$, and they yield the sequence of *state transition*. The network begins the state transition once it is initialized at instant 0 with $\mathbf{x}^0$, and it goes through state transitions $\mathbf{o}^k$, for $k = 1, 2, \ldots$, until it possibly finds an equilibrium state. This equilibrium state is often called an *attractor*. An attractor can consist of a single state or a limited number of states [4].

2.3 NEURAL PROCESSING

The process of computation of $\mathbf{o}$ for a given $\mathbf{x}$ performed by the network is known as *recall*. Recall is the proper processing phase for a neural network, and its objective is to retrieve the information. Recall corresponds to the encoding of the stored content which may have been encoded in a network previously [4].

If we assume that a set of patterns can be stored in the network. Later, if the network is presented with a pattern similar to a member of the stored set, it may associate the input with the closest stored pattern. The process is called *autoassociation*. Typically, a degraded input pattern serves as a cue for retrieval of its original form. This illustrated schematically in Figure 2.3(a).

Association of input patterns can also be stored in a *heteroassociation* variant. In heteroassociation processing, the association between pairs of patterns are stored. This is schematically shown in Figure 2.3(b). A square input pattern presented at the input results in the rhomboid at the output. It can be inferred that the rhomboid and square constitute one pair of stored patterns. A distorted input pattern may causes also correct heteroassociation at the output as shown with dashed line.

Classification is another form of neural computation. Let us assume that a set of input patterns is divided into a number of classes, or categories. In response to an input pattern from the set, the classifier is supposed to recall the information regarding class membership of the input pattern. Typically, classes are expressed by discrete-valued output vectors, and thus output neurons of classifier would employ binary activation functions. The schematic diagram illustrating the classification response for patterns belonging to three classes is shown in Figure 2.4(a).

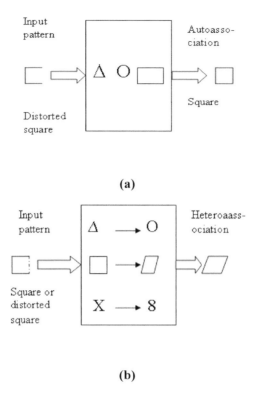

Figure 2.3 Association response: (a) autoassociation and (b) heteroassociation

Interestingly, classification can be understood as a special case of heteroassociation [4]. The association is now between the input pattern and the second member of the heteroassociative pair, which is supposed to indicate the input's class number. If the input desired response is the class number but the input pattern does not exactly correspond to any of the patterns in the set, the processing is called *recognition*. When a class membership for one of the patterns in the set is recalled, recognition becomes identical to classification. Recognition within the set of three patterns is schematically shown in Figure 2.4(b). This form of processing is of particular significance when an amount of noise is superimposed on input patterns.

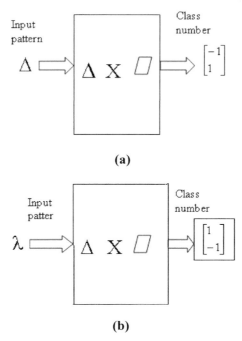

Figure 2.4: Classification response (a) classification and (b) recognition

2.4 LEARNING AND ADAPTATION

In general, learning is a relatively permanent change in behavior brought about by experience. Learning in neural networks is a more direct process, and we typically can capture each learning step in a distinct cause-effect relation. To performing any of the processing tasks discussed in the previous section, neural network learning of an input-output mapping from a set of examples needed. Designing an associator or a classifier can be based on learning a relationship that transforms inputs into outputs given a set of examples of input-output pairs. A classical framework for this problem is provided by approximation theory.

2.5 NEURAL NETWORK LEARNING RULES

A neuron is considered to be an adaptive element. Its weights are modifiable depending on the input signal it receives, its output value, and the associated teacher response. In some cases the teacher signal is not available and no error information can be used, thus the neuron will modify its weights based only on the input and / or output. This is the case for unsupervised learning [4].

This section will cover single-neuron and single-layer network supervised learning and simple case of unsupervised learning. Under different learning rules, the form of the neuron's activation function may be different. Note that the threshold parameter may be included in learning as one of the weights. This requires fixing one of the inputs, say x_n. We will assume here that x_n, if fixed, takes the value of -1.

The following *general rule* is adopted in neural network studies: *The weight vector* $\mathbf{w_i} = [\ w_{i1}\ w_{i2}\ ...\ w_{in}\ ]^T$ *increases in proportion to the product of input* $\mathbf{x}$ *and learning signal* r. The learning signal r is in general a function of $\mathbf{w_i}$, $\mathbf{x}$, and sometimes of the teacher's signal d_i. Thus we have

$$r = f(\mathbf{w_i}, \mathbf{x}, d_i) \qquad (2.11)$$

The incremental of the weight vector $\mathbf{w_i}$ produced by the learning step at time t according to the general learning rule is [4]

$$\Delta \mathbf{w}_i(t) = cr\,[\mathbf{w}_i(t), \mathbf{x}(t), d_i(t)\,]\,\mathbf{x}(t) \qquad (2.12)$$

where c is a positive number called the *learning constant* that determines the rate of learning. The weight vector adapted at time t becomes at the next instant or learning step

$$\mathbf{w}_i(t+1) = \mathbf{w}_i(t) + cr\,[\mathbf{w}_i(t), \mathbf{x}(t), d_i(t)]\,\mathbf{x}(t) \qquad (2.13a)$$

The superscript convention will be used in this text to index the discrete-time training steps as in Eq. (2.13a). For the kth step we have

$$\mathbf{w}_i^{k+1} = \mathbf{w}_i^k + cr(\mathbf{w}_i^k, \mathbf{x}^k, d_i^k)\mathbf{x}^k \qquad (2.13b)$$

The learning in (2.13) assumes the form of a sequence of discrete-time weight modifications. Continuous-time can be expressed as

$$\frac{dw_i(t)}{dt} = crx(t) \qquad (2.14)$$

Discrete-time, or stepwise, learning is reviewed below. Weights are assumed to have been suitably initialized before each learning experiment started.

2.5.1 HEBBIAN LEARNING RULE

For the Hebbian learning rule the learning signal is equal simply to the neuron's output [4]. We have

$$r = f(\mathbf{w}_i^T \mathbf{x}) \qquad (2.15)$$

The incremental $\Delta \mathbf{w}_i$ of the weight vector becomes

$$\Delta \mathbf{w}_i = cf(\mathbf{w}_i^T \mathbf{x})\mathbf{x} \qquad (2.16a)$$

The single weight w_{ij} is adapted using the following increment:

$$\Delta \mathbf{w}_i = cf(\mathbf{w}_i^T \mathbf{x})x_j \qquad (2.16b)$$

This can be written briefly as

$$\Delta \mathbf{w}_i = co_i x_j \qquad (2.16c)$$

This learning rule requires the weight initialization at small random values around $\mathbf{w}_i = \mathbf{0}$ prior to learning. The Hebbian learning rule represents a purely feedforward, unsupervised learning. The rule element the interpretation of the classic statement: "When an axon cell A is near enough to excite a cell B and repeatedly or persistently takes place in firing it, some growth process or metabolic change take place in one or both cells such that A's efficiency, as one of the cells firing B, is increased,".

The rule states that if the crossproduct of output and input, or correlation term $o_i x_j$ is positive, this results in an increase of weight w_{ij}; otherwise the weight decreases. It can be seen that the output is strengthened in turn for each input presented. Therefore, frequent input pattern will have most influence at the neuron's weight vector and will eventually produce the largest output [4].

2.5.2 PERCEPTRON LEARNING RULE

For perceptron learning rule, the learning signal is the difference between the desired and actual neuron's response. Thus, learning is supervised and the learning signal is equal to

$$r = d_i - o_i \qquad (2.17)$$

where $o_i = sgn(\mathbf{w}^T \mathbf{x})$, and d_i is the desired response. Weight adjustments in this method, $\Delta \mathbf{w}_i$ and Δw_{ij} are obtained as follows

$$\Delta \mathbf{w}_i = c[d_i - o_i]\, \mathbf{x} \qquad (2.18a)$$
$$\Delta w_{ij} = c[d_i - o_i]\, x_j \qquad \text{for } j = 1, 2, ..., n \qquad (2.18b)$$

Note that this rule is applicable only for binary neuron response, and the relationships (2.18) express the rule for the bipolar binary case [4]. Under this rule, weights are adjusted if and only if o_i is incorrect. Error as a necessary condition of learning is inherently include in this training (2.18a) reduces to

$$\Delta \mathbf{w_i} = \pm 2cx \quad (2.19)$$

where a plus sign is applicable when $d_i = 1$, and $sgn(\mathbf{w}^T\mathbf{x}) = -1$, and a minus sign is applicable when $d_i = -1$, and $sgn(\mathbf{w}^T\mathbf{x}) = 1$. Notice that the weight adjustment formula (2.19) cannot be used when $d_i = sgn(\mathbf{w}^T\mathbf{x})$. The weight adjustment is inherently zero when the desired and actual responses agree. The perceptron learning rule is of central importance for supervised learning of neural networks. The weights are initialized at any values in this method.

2.5.3 DELTA LEARNING RULE

The delta learning rule is only valid for continuous activation function as defined in (2.20a), (2.20b), and in the supervised training method.

$$f(net) = \frac{2}{1+\exp(-\lambda net)} - 1 \quad (2.20a)$$

$$f(net) = \frac{1}{1+\exp(-\lambda net)} \quad (2.20b)$$

The learning signal for this rule is called *delta* and is defined as follows

$$r = [\ d_i - f(\mathbf{w}^T_i\mathbf{x})\ ]f'(\mathbf{w}^T_i\mathbf{x}) \quad (2.21)$$

The term $f'(\mathbf{w}^T_i\mathbf{x})$ is the derivative of the activation function $f(net)$ computed for $net = \mathbf{w}^T_i\mathbf{x}$. This learning rule can be readily derived from the condition of least squared error between o_i and d_i. Calculating the gradient vector w_i^{th} to $\mathbf{w_i}$ of the squared error defined as

$$E = \frac{1}{2}(d_i - o_i)^2 \qquad (2.22)$$

Considering the use of the general learning rule (2.12) and plugging in the learning signal as defined in (2.21), the weight adjustment becomes

$$\Delta \mathbf{w_i} = c(d_i - o_i)f'(net_i)\mathbf{x} \qquad (2.23)$$

The weights are initialized at any values for this method of training. This rule also can be called the continuous perceptron training rule [4].

2.5.4 WIDROW-HOFF LEARNING RULE

The Widrow-Hoff learning rule is applicable for the supervised training of neural networks. It is independent of the activation function of neurons used since it minimizes the squared error between the desired output value d_i and the neuron's activation value $net_i = \mathbf{w}^T_i\mathbf{x}$. The learning signal for this rule is defined as follows

$$r = d_i - \mathbf{w}^T_i\mathbf{x} \qquad (2.24)$$

The weight vector increment under this learning rule is

$$\Delta \mathbf{w_i} = c(d_i - \mathbf{w}^T_i\mathbf{x})\mathbf{x} \qquad (2.25a)$$

or, for the single weight the adjustment is

$$\Delta w_{ij} = c(d_i - \mathbf{w}^T_i\mathbf{x})x_j \qquad (2.25b)$$

This rule can be considered a special case of the delta learning rule. Indeed, assuming in (2.21) that $f(\mathbf{w}^T_i\mathbf{x}) = \mathbf{w}^T_i\mathbf{x}$, or the activation function is simply the identity function $f(net) = net$, we obtain $f'(net) = 1$, and (2.21) becomes identical to (2.24). Weights are initialized at any values in this method [4].

2.5.5 CORRELATION LEARNING RULE

By substituting $r = d_i$ into the general learning rule (2.12) we obtain the correlation learning rule. The adjustment for the weight vector and the single weights, respectively, are

$$\Delta \mathbf{w}_i = c d_i \mathbf{x} \qquad (2.26a)$$

$$\Delta w_{ij} = c d_i x_j \qquad (2.26b)$$

This simple rule states that if d_i is the desired response due to x_j, the corresponding weight increase is proportional to their product. The rule typically applies to recording data in memory networks with binary response neurons. Correlation rule is performed in supervised environment and requires the weight initialization $\mathbf{w} = \mathbf{0}$.

2.5.6 WINNER-TAKE-ALL LEARNING RULE

This learning differs substantially from any of the rules discussed so far in this section. It can only be demonstrated and explained for an ensemble of neurons, preferably arranged in a layer of p units. This rule is an example of competitive learning, and it is used for unsupervised network training. Typically, winner-take-all learning is used for learning statistical properties of inputs [4]. The learning is based on the premise that one of the neurons in the layer, say the m'th, has the maximum response due to input $\mathbf{x}$. This neuron is declared the *winner*. As a result of this winning event, the weight vector $\mathbf{w}_m$

$$\mathbf{w}_m = [w_{m1} \ w_{m2} \ \ldots \ w_{mn}]^T \qquad (2.27)$$

The increment is computed as follows

$$\Delta w_m = \alpha \, (x - w_m) \qquad (2.28a)$$

or, the individual weight adjustment becomes

$$\Delta w_{mj} = \alpha(x_j - w_{mj}), \qquad \text{for } j = 1, 2, \ldots, n \qquad (2.28b)$$

where α > 0 is a small learning constant, typically decreasing as learning progress. The winner selection is based on the following criterion of maximum activation among all p neurons participating in a competition:

$$w^T_m x = max\ (w^T_i x) \qquad \text{for } I = 1, 2, ..., p \qquad (2.29)$$

Note that only the winning neuron fan-in weight vector is adjusted. After adjustment, its fan-in weights tend to better estimate the input pattern in question. Weights are typically initialized at random values and their lengths are normalized during learning in this method [4].

2.5.7 OUTSTAR LEARNING RULE

Outstar learning rule is another learning rule that is best explained when neurons are arranged in a layer [4]. This rule is designed to produce a desired response **d** of the layer of p neurons. The rule is used to provide learning of repetitive and characteristic properties of input / output relationships. This rule is concerned with supervised learning; however, it supposed to allow the network to extract statistical properties of the input and output signals. The weight adjustment in this rule are computed as follows [4]

$$\Delta w_j = \beta(d - w_j) \qquad (2.30a)$$

or, the individual weight adjustments are

$$\Delta w_{mj} = \beta(d_m - w_m), \qquad \text{for } m = 1, 2, ..., p \qquad (2.30b)$$

Weight vector in (2.30a) is defined accordingly as

$$\mathbf{w}_j = [\ w_{1j}\ w_{2j}\ ...\ w_{pj}\ ]^T \qquad (2.31)$$

Arbitrarily selectable β is a small positive learning constant decreasing during training. The rule typically ensure that the output pattern becomes similar to the undistorted desired output after repetitively applying (2.30) on distorted output versions.

2.6 SUMMARY

In this chapter the recall networks can be performed in the feedforward mode, or from input toward output, only. Such networks are called feedforward and have no memory. Feedforward network's behavior does not depend on what happened in the past but what happens now. The second group of networks performed recall computation with feedback operational. Feedback networks are also called recurrent. They interact with their input through the output. Recurrent networks can operate either in a discrete- or continuous- time mode.

Seven learning rules are compared in terms of the single weight adjustment formula, supervised versus unsupervised learning mode, weight initialization, and required neuron activation functions. Most learning rule allows for learning of a single, isolated neuron's weight with exception of winner-take-all and outstar rules. Both of these rules require layer neurons in order for the weight adaptation to proceed.

CHAPTER 3

TIME SERIES PROCESSING USING NEURAL NETWORKS

3.1 INTRODUCTION

Neural networks, being developed primarily for the purpose of pattern recognition (classification), are not well suited for modeling time series because the original applications of neural networks were concerned with detection of patterns in arrays of measurements which do not change in time [5].The dynamic nature of spatio-temporal data (i.e. data that has a spatial and a temporal dimension) as time series are, requires introduction of additional mechanisms. In particular, a neural network used for time series processing must possess memory in one way or the other.

One way to supply the neural network with memory is to use a *time window*. In this case, a certain number of past time series elements is provided to the network as inputs and the network produces a prediction of the next element.

Another way to provide memory to the neural network is to store past values of output (context layer) or hidden (state layer) nodes in additional layers. These additional layers are connected to the hidden layer in a similar way as the input layer.

3.2 MULTI-LAYER FEEDFORWARD

In general, the layered network is mapping the input vector **z** into the output vector **o** as follows

$$o = N[z] \qquad (3.1)$$

where N denote a composite nonlinear matrix operator. For the two-layer network, the mapping **z** to **o** as in (3.1) can be represented as a mapping within a mapping, or

$$o = \Gamma[W\Gamma[Vz]] \qquad (3.2a)$$

where the internal mapping is

$$\Gamma[Vz] = y \qquad (3.2b)$$

and it related to the hidden layer mapping **z** to **y**. Note that each of the mapping is performed by a single-layer of the layered network [4]. The operator Γ is a nonlinear diagonal operator with diagonal elements being identical activation function as in (3.3). The diagonal elements of Γ operator on *net* values produced at inputs of each neuron. It follows from (3.2) that the $f(\cdot)$ arguments here are elements of vectors **net**$_j$ and **net**$_k$ for the hidden and output layers, respectively.

$$o = \Gamma[Wy] \qquad (3.3)$$

As can be seen from (3.2), the assumption of identical and fixed activation functions $f(net)$ leads to the conclusion that the only parameters for mapping **z** to **o** so that **o** matches **d** are weights. Specifically, we have two matrices **V** and **W** to be adjusted so that the error value proportional to $\|\mathbf{d} - \mathbf{o}\|^2$ is minimized. Thus, we can look at layered neural networks as versatile nonlinear mapping systems with weights serving as parameters.

3.2.1 ERROR BACK-PROPAGATION TRAINING

Figure 3.1 illustrates the flowchart of the error back-propagation training algorithm for a basic two-layer network. The learning begins with the feedforward recall phase (step 2). After a single pattern vector **z** is submitted at the input, the layers' responses **y** and **o** are computed in this phase [4]. Then, the error signal computation phase (step 4) follows. Note that the error signal vector must be determined in the output layer first, and then it is propagated toward the network input nodes. As in Figure (3.2) the $K \times J$ weights are subsequently adjusted within the matrix **W** in step 5. Finally, $J \times I$ weights are adjusted within the matrix **V** in step 6. Note that the cumulative cycle error of input to output mapping is computed in step 3 as a sum over all continuous output errors in the entire training set. The final error value for the entire training cycle is calculated after each completed pass through the training set $\{z_1, z_2, ..., z_p\}$. The learning procedure stops when the final error value below the upper bound, E_{max}, is obtained as shown in step 8 [4].

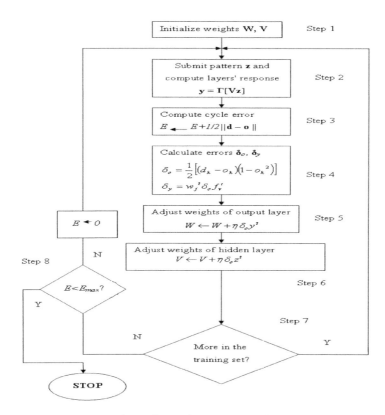

Figure 3.1: Flowchart of error back-propagation training algorithm.

The algorithm of error back-propagation training is given below.

Figure 3.2: Summary of the Error Back-Propagation Training Algorithm (EBPTA)

Given are p training pairs

$$\{z_1, d_1, d_2, ..., z_p, d_p\}$$

where z_i is $(I \times 1)$, d_i is $(K \times 1)$, and $i = 1, 2, ..., P$. Note that the $I'th$ component of each z_i is of value -1 since input vectors have been augmented. Since $J - 1$ of the hidden layer having outputs y selected. Note that the $J'th$ component of y is of value -1, since hidden layer outputs have also been augmented; y is $(J \times 1)$ and o is $(K \times 1)$.

<u>Step 1:</u> $\eta > 0$, E_{max} chosen.

Weights W and V are initialized at small random values; W is $(K \times J)$, V is $(J \times I)$.

$$q \leftarrow 1, p \leftarrow 1, E \leftarrow 0$$

<u>Step 2:</u> Training step starts here(See not 1 at end of list)

Input is presented and the layers' outputs computed [$f(net)$ as in (2.20a) is used]:

$$z \leftarrow z_p, d \leftarrow d_p$$

$$y_j \leftarrow f(v'_j z), \quad \text{for } j = 1, 2, ..., J$$

where v_j, a column vector, is the $j'th$ row of V, and

$$o_k \leftarrow f(w'_k y), \quad \text{for } k = 1, 2, ..., K$$

where w_k, a column vector, is the $k'th$ row of W.

<u>Step 3:</u>   Error value is computed:

$$E \leftarrow \frac{1}{2}(d_k - o_k)^2 + E, \quad \text{for } k = 1, 2, ..., K$$

<u>Step 4:</u>   Error signal vectors δ_o and δ_y of both layers are computed. Vector δ_o is $(K \times 1)$, δ_y is $(J \times 1)$. The error signal terms of the output layer in this step are:

$$\delta_{ok} = \frac{1}{2}(d_k - o_k)(1 - o_k^2), \qquad \text{for } k = 1, 2, ..., K$$

The error signal terms of the hidden layer in this step are

$$\delta_{yj} = \frac{1}{2}(1 - y_j^2)\sum_{k=1}^{K} \delta_{ok} w_{kj}, \qquad \text{for } j = 1, 2, ..., J$$

Step 5: Output layer weights are adjusted:

$$w_{kj} \leftarrow w_{kj} + \eta \delta_{ok} y_j, \qquad \text{for } k = 1, 2, ..., K \text{ and}$$
$$j = 1, 2, ..., J$$

Step 6: Hidden layer weights are adjusted:

$$v_{ji} \leftarrow v_{ji} + \eta \delta_{yj} z_i, \qquad \text{for } j = 1, 2, ..., J \text{ and}$$
$$i = 1, 2, ..., I$$

Step 7: If $p < P$ then $p \leftarrow p+1, q \leftarrow q+1$, and go to Step 2; otherwise, go to Step 8.

Step 8: The training cycle is completed.
For $E < E_{max}$, then terminate the training session. Output weights **W**, **V**, q, and E.
If $E > E_{max}$, then E 0, p 1, and initiate the new training cycle by going to Step 2.

Note 1: For best results, patterns should be chosen at random from the training set.

Note 2: If formula (2.20b) is used in Step 2, then the error signal terms in Step 4 are computed as follows

$$\delta_{ok} = (d_k - o_k)(1 - o_k)o_k, \qquad \text{for } k = 1, 2, ..., K$$

$$\delta_{yj} = y_j(1 - y_j)\sum_{k=1}^{K} \delta_{ok} w_{kj}, \qquad \text{for } j = 1, 2, ..., J$$

Chapter 3

Time series processing using neural networks

Several aspects of the back-propagation training method are noteworthy. The incremental learning of the weight matrix in the output and hidden layers is obtained by the outer product rule as

$$\Delta W = \eta \delta y^T \tag{3.4}$$

where δ is the error signal vector of a layer and **y** is the input signal vector to that layer. Noticeably, the error signal components δ_{ok} at the output layer are obtained as simple scalar products of the output error component $d_k - o_k$ and $f'(net_k)$. In contrast to this mode of error computation, hidden-layer error signal components δ_{yj} are computed with the weight matrix **W** seen in the feedforward mode, but now using its column $\mathbf{w}_j$. As we realize, the feedforward mode involves rows of matrix **W** for the computation of the following layer's response [4].

Another observation can be made regarding linear versus nonlinear operation of the network during training and recall phases. Although the network is nonlinear in the feedforward mode, the error back-propagation is computed using the linearized activation function.

Finally, Multi layer perceptron neural networks can be used for time series processing. If such a network has the architecture shown in Figure 3.3 where the individual input nodes are "connected" to the elements of the time series 1, 2,... , p steps in the past.

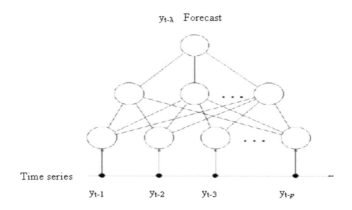

Figure 3.3: A feedforward neural network with time window

3.2.2 LEARNING FACTORS

The back-propagation learning algorithm in which synaptic strengths are systematically modified so that the response of the network increasingly approximates the desired response can be interpreted as an optimization problem. The generic criterion function optimization algorithm is simply negative gradient descent with a fixed step size. The learning algorithm modifies the weight matrices so that the error value decreases [4].

The essence of the error back-propagation algorithm is the evaluation of the contribution of each particular weight to the output error. There are several main aspects and some practical properties of error back-propagation algorithm. The most important of these are initial weights, cumulative weight adjustment, the form of the neuron's activation function, and selection of the learning constant.

3.2.2.1 INITIAL WEIGHTS

The weights of the network to be trained are typically initialized at small random values. The initialization strongly affects the ultimate solution. If all weights start out with equal weight values, and if the solution requires that unequal weights be developed, the network may not trained properly. Unless the network is disturbed by random factors of the random character of input patterns during training, the internal representation may continuously result in symmetric weights.

Also, the network may fail to learn the set of training examples with the error stabilizing or even increasing as the learning continues. In fact, many empirical studies of the algorithm point out the continuing training beyond a certain low-error plateau results in the undesirable drift of weights. This causes the error to increase and the quality of mapping implemented by the network decreases. To counteract the drift problem, network learning should be restarted with other random weights. The choice of initial weights is, however, only one of several factors affecting the training of the network toward an acceptable error minimum [4].

3.2.2.2 CUMULATIVE WEIGHT ADJUSTMENT VERSUS INCREMENTAL UPDATING

The error back-propagation learning based on the single pattern error reduction requires a small adjustment of weights which follows each presentation of the training pattern. This scheme is called *incremental updating*. The back-propagation learning also implements the gradient-like descent minimization of the overall error function computed over the complete cycle of P presentation provided the learning constant η is sufficiently small.

The network trained, however, may be skewed toward the most recent patterns in the cycle. To counteract this specific problem, either a small learning constant η should be used or cumulative weight changes imposed as follows

$$\Delta w = \sum_{p=1}^{P} \Delta w_p \qquad (3.5)$$

for both output and hidden layers. The weight adjustment in this scheme is implemented at the conclusion of the complete learning cycle. This may also have an averaging effect on the training, however. Provided that the learning constant is small enough, the cumulative weight adjustment procedure can still implement the algorithm close to the gradient descent minimization [4].

Although either cumulative weight adjustment after each completed training cycle or incremental weight adjustment after each single pattern presentation can bring satisfactory solutions, attention should be paid to the fact that the training works best under random conditions.

3.2.2.3 STEEPNESS OF THE ACTIVATION FUNCTION

The neuron's continuous activation function $f(net, \lambda)$ is characterized by its steepness factor λ. Also, the derivative $f'(net)$ of the activation function serves as a multiplying factor in building components of the error signal vectors δ_o and δ_y. Thus, both the choice and shape of the activation function would strongly affect the speed of network learning.

$$f(net) = \frac{2}{1 + \exp(-\lambda net)} - 1 \qquad (3.6)$$

The derivative of the activation function (3.4) can be easily computed as follows

$$f'(net) = \frac{2\lambda \exp(-\lambda net)}{[1+\exp(-\lambda net)]^2} \qquad (3.7)$$

Since weights are adjusted in proportion to the value $f'(net)$, the weights that are connected to units responding in their midrange are changed the most. The weights of uncommitted neurons with uncertain responses are thus affected more strongly than those neurons that already heavily turned on or turned off. Since the local signal errors δ_{ok} and δ_{yj} are computed with $f'(net)$ as a multiplier, the transmitted components of the back-propagating error are large only for neurons in steep thresholding mode [4].

Also, for fixed learning constant all adjustments of weights are in proportion to the steepness coefficient λ. This particular observation leads are to the conclusion that using activation functions with large λ may yield results similar as the case of large learning constant η. It thus seems advisable to keep λ at a standard value of 1, and to control the learning speed using solely the learning constant η, rather than controlling both η and λ.

3.2.2.4 LEARNING CONSTANT

The effectiveness and convergence of the error back-propagation learning algorithm depend significantly on the value of the learning constant η. In general, however, the optimum value of η depends on the problem being solved, and there is no single learning constant value suitable for different training cases. This problem seems to be common for all gradient-based optimization schemes. While gradient descent can be an efficient method for obtaining the weight values that minimize an error, error surfaces frequently possess properties that make the procedure slow to converge.

When broad minima yield small gradient values, then a larger value of η will result in a more rapid convergence. However, for problem with steep and narrow minima, a small value of η must be chosen to avoid overshooting the solution. This leads to the conclusion that η should indeed be chosen experimentally for each problem. One should also remember that only small learning constants guarantee a true gradient descent. The price of this guarantee is an increased total number of learning steps that need to be made to reach the satisfactory solution.

Although the choice of the learning constant depends strongly on the class of the learning problem and on the network architecture, the value ranging from 10^{-3} to 10 have been reported throughout the technical literature as successful for many computational back-propagation experiments. For large learning constants, the learning speed can be drastically increased; however, the learning may not be exact, with tendencies to overshoot, or it may never stabilize at any minimum.

3.3 TIME-DELAY NEURAL NETWORK

Another mechanism to supply neural networks with"memory" to deal with the temporal dimension is the introduction of time delays on connections. In other words, through delays, inputs arrive at hidden units at different points in time, thus being "stored" long enough to influence subsequent inputs. This approach, called a *time-delay neural network* (TDNN) has been extensively employed in speech recognition. Formally, time delays are identical to time windows and can thus be viewed as autoregressive models as well. An interesting extension is the introduction of time delays also on connections between hidden and output units, providing additional, more "abstract" memory to the network [6].

3.4 JORDAN NETWORK

Figure 3.4 shows another approach for processing time series using neural networks, the so-called *Jordan* network. It is a multi-layer perceptron with one hidden layer and a feedback loop from the output layer to an additional input layer called *context layer*. Each node in the context layer is connected to itself via self-recurrent loops with a weight smaller than 1.

Hence, a Jordan network takes into account not only past time series elements, but also its own forecasts. This property has often given rise to the argument that recurrent networks can exploit information beyond a limited time window. However, in practice this cannot really be exploited. If the weight of a connection to a context node is close to 1, the node (if it uses a sigmoid transfer function) quickly saturates to maximum activation, where additional inputs have little effect. If the weight is very small in comparison to 1, the influence of past estimates quickly goes to 0 [6].

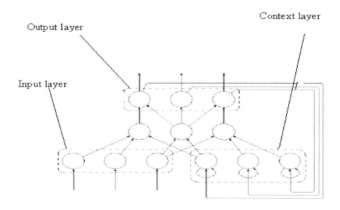

Figure 3.4: Jordan network

3.5 ELMAN NETWORK

An Elman network figure 3.5 possesses an additional layer called *state layer*, by means of which the outputs of the hidden nodes are fed back to the network. Although the Elman network in the original form has only limited modeling capabilities, it can be extended to perform as a universal state-space model which describes and forecasts time series under the assumption that the next element of the time series can be predicted by the state the system currently is in, no matter how the state was reached. All the history of the series necessary for producing the next element can be expressed by one state vector [6].

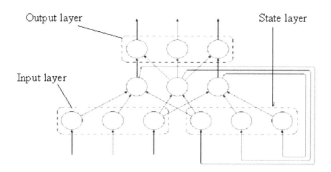

Figure 3.5: Elman network

3.6 MULTI-RECURRENT NETWORK

This type of neural network has several remarkable properties. Firstly, feedback from hidden *and* output layers is permitted. Secondly, all input layers (the actual input, the state and the context layer) are permitted to be extended by time-delays, such as to introduce time windows over past instances of the corresponding vectors. Thirdly, like in the Jordan network, self-recurrent loops in the state layer can be introduced. The weights of these loops, and the weights of the feedback copies resulting from the recurrent one-to-one connections, are chosen such as to scale the theoretically maximum input to each unit in the state layer 1, and to give more or less weight to the feedback connections of the self-recurrent loops, respectively [6].

If, for example, 75 % of the total activation of a unit in the state layer comes from the hidden layer feedback, and 25 % comes from self-recurrency, the state layer will tend to change considerably at each time step. If, on the other hand, only 25 % come from the hidden layer feedback, and 75 % from the self-recurrent loops the state vector will tend to remain similar to the one at the previous time step.

By introducing several state layers with different such weighting schemes, the network can exploit both the information of rather recent time steps and a kind of average of several past time steps, i.e. a longer, averaged history.

It is clear that a full-fletched version of the MRN contains a very large number of parameters (weights) and requires even more care than the other models discussed above. Several empirical studies [7] have shown, however, that for real-world applications, some versions of the MRN can significantly outperform most other, more simple, forecasting methods.

Another advantage of self-recurrent loops becomes evident in applications where patterns in the time series can vary in time scale. This phenomenon is called *time warping*, and is especially known in speech recognition, where different speech patterns can vary in length and relationships between segments dependent on speaking speed and intonation [8]. In autoregressive models with fixed time windows, such distorted patterns lead to vectors that do not share sufficient similarities to be classified correctly. This is sometimes called the *temporal invariance problem* - the problem of recognizing temporal patterns independent of their duration and temporal distortion. In a recurrent neural network with self-recurrent loops such invariances can be dealt with, especially when sluggish state spaces are employed. If state vector is forced to be similar at subsequent time steps, events can be treated equally (or similarly) even when they are shifted along temporal dimension [6].

3.7 OTHER NETWORK ARCHITECTURES

While the most important neural network approaches to time series processing have been described in previous sections, there exists a variety of many other design approaches, several of which are listed below [6]:

- Many time series applications are tackled with *fully recurrent networks*, or networks with recurrent architectures different from the ones already discussed. Special learning algorithms for arbitrary recurrent networks have been devised, such as *backpropagation in time* and real-time recurrent learning.
- Many authors use a combination of neural networks with so-called *hidden Markov models* (HMM) for time series and signal processing. HMMs are related to finite state automata and describe probabilities for changing from one state to the other.
- Unsupervised neural network learning algorithms, such as the self-organizing map, can also be applied in time series processing, both in forecasting and classification. The latter application constitutes an instance of so-called *spatiotemporal clustering*, i.e. the unsupervised classification

of time series into clusters - in this case the clustering of sleep-EEG into sleep stages [5].

3.8 SUMMARY

In this chapter it was defined what a time series signal is and what are its basic properties. The architecture of multi-layer feedforward was also presented. Following, error back-propagation algorithm and their properties was outlined in details. Finally, some other architecture using in time series processing are also presented.

CHAPTER 4

DESIGN OF ANN IN TIME SERIES

4.1 INTRODUCTION

The design of a neural network successfully predicting time series is a complex task. In this chapter, the individual steps used to solve the time series prediction problem are presented.

4.2 VARIABLE SELECTION

Success in designing a neural network depends on a clear understanding of the problem. Technical inputs are defined as lagged "an element of the time series in the past" values of the dependent variable "the variable whose behavior should be modeled or predicted" or indicators calculated from the lagged values. The simplest neural network model uses lagged values of the dependent variable(s) or its first difference as inputs. A more popular approach is to calculate various technical indicators which are based only on past of the time series being forecasted.

4.3 DATA COLLECTION

The researcher must consider cost and availability when collecting data for the variables chosen in the previous step. Technical data is readily available from many vendors at a reasonable cost whereas fundamental information is more difficult to obtain. Time spent collecting data cannot be used for preprocessing, training and evaluating network performance. The vendor should have a reputation of providing high quality data; however, all data should still be checked for errors by examining day to day changes, ranges, logical consistency (e.g. high greater than or equal to close, open greater or equal to low) and missing observations [9].

Missing observations which often exist can be handled in a number of ways. All missing observations can be dropped or a second option is to assume that the missing observations remain the same by interpolating or averaging from nearby values. Dedicating an input neuron to the missing observations by coding it as a one if missing and zero otherwise is also often done. When using fundamental data as an input in a neural network four issues must be kept in mind. First, the method of calculating the fundamental indicator should be consistent over the time series. Second, the data should not have been retroactively revised after its initial publication as is commonly done in databases since the revised numbers are not available in actual forecasting. Third, the data must be appropriately lagged as an input in the neural network since fundamental information is not available. Fourth, the researcher should be confident, that the source will continue to publish the particular fundamental information or other identical sources are available [9].

4.4 DATA PREPROCESSING

As in most other neural network applications, data preprocessing is crucial for achieving a good prediction performance when applying neural networks for time series prediction. The input and output variables for which the data was collected are rarely fed into the network in raw form. At the very least, the raw data must be scaled between the upper and lower bounds of the transfer functions (usually between zero and one or minus one and one; [9]).

Two of the most common data transformations in both traditional and neural network forecasting are first differencing and taking log" logarithm" of a variable. First differencing, or using changes in a variable, can be used to remove a linear trend from the data. Logarithmic transformation is useful for data which can take on both small and large values. Logarithmic transformations also convert multiplicative or ratio relationships to additive which is believed to simplify and improve the network training.

Another popular data transformation is to use ratios of input variables. Ratios highlight important relationships while at the same time conserving degrees of freedom because fewer input neurons are required to code the independent variables. Besides first differences, logs and ratios, technical analysis can provide a neural network with a wealth of indicators including a variety of moving averages, oscillators, directional movement and volatility filters. It is a good idea to use mix of different indicators to reduce variable redundancy and provide network with the ability to adapt to changing conditions through periodic retraining [9].

Smoothing both input and output data by using either simple or exponential moving averages is often employed. Using moving averages to smooth the independent variables and forecasting trends may be a more promising approach [9]. Sampling or filtering of data refers to removing observations from the training and testing sets to create a more uniform distribution. The type of filtering employed should be consistent with the objectives of the researcher. The network minimizes the sum of squared errors (or other error function) over all the training facts. The researcher must be clear on what exactly the neural network is supposed to learn. Another advantage of filtering is a decrease in the number of training facts which allows testing of more input variables, random starting weights or hidden neurons rather than training large data sets.

In practice, data preprocessing involves much trial and error. One method to select appropriate input variables is to test various combinations. For example, a "top 20" list of variables consisting of a variety of technical indicators could be pretested ten at a time with each combination differing by two or three variables. Although computationally intensive, this procedure recognizes the likelihood that some variables may be excellent predictors only when in combination with other variables.

4.5 DATA PARTITIONING

Common practice is to divide the time series into three distinct sets called the training, testing and validation (out-of-sample) sets. The training set is the largest set and is used by the neural network to learn the patterns present in the data. The testing set, ranging in size from 10 % to 30 % of the training set, is used to evaluate the generalization ability of a supposedly trained network. The researcher would select the network(s) which perform best on the testing set. A final check on the validation set chosen must strike a balance between obtaining a sufficient sample size to evaluate a trained network and having enough remaining observations for both training and testing. The validation set should consist of the most recent contiguous observations. Care must be taken not to use the validation set as a testing set by repeatedly performing a series of train test-validation steps and adjusting the input variables based on the network's performance on the validation set [9].

The testing set can be either randomly selected from the training set or consist of a set of observations immediately following the training set. The testing set will favor networks which specialize on strong uptrends at the expense of networks which generalize by performing well on both uptrends and downtrends. The advantage of using the observations following the training set as testing facts is that these are the most recent observations (excluding the validation set) which may be more important than older data [9].

The randomly selected testing facts should not be replaced in the training set because this would bias the ability to evaluate generalization especially if the testing set is large relative to the training set (e.g. 30 %). A deterministic method, such as selecting every n_{th} observation as a testing fact, is also not recommended since it can result in cycles in the sampled data due solely to the sampling technique employed.

A more rigorous approach in evaluating neural networks is to use a *walk-forward testing* routine also known as either *sliding* or *moving window* testing. Popular in evaluating commodity trading systems, walk-forward testing involves dividing the data into a series of overlapping training-testing-validation sets. Each set is moved forward through the time series. Walkforward testing attempts to simulate real-life trading and tests the robustness of the model through its frequent retraining on a large out-of-sample data set.

In walk-forward testing, the size of the validation set drives the retraining frequency of the neural network. Frequent retraining is more time consuming, but allows the network to adapt more quickly to changing market conditions. The consistency or variation of the results in the out-of-sample sets is an important performance measure [9].

4.6 NEURAL NETWORK DESIGN

There are an infinite number of ways to construct a neural network. *Neurodynamics* and *architecture* are two terms used to describe the way in which a neural network is organized. The combination of neurodynamics and architecture define the neural networks's *paradigm*. Neurodynamics describe the properties of an individual neuron such as its transfer function and how the inputs are combined [10]. A neural network's architecture defines its structures including the number of neurons in each layer and the number and type of interconnections. The number of input neurons is one of the easiest parameters to select once the independent variables have been preprocessed because each independent variable is represented by its own input neuron. The tasks of selection of the number of hidden layers, the number of neurons in the hidden layers, the number of output neurons as well as the transfer functions are much more difficult [9].

4.6.1 NUMBER OF HIDDEN NEURONS

Despite its importance, there is no "magic" formula for selecting the optimum number of hidden neurons. Therefore researchers fall back on experimentation. However, some rules of thumb have been advanced. A rough approximation can be obtained by the geometric pyramid rule proposed by Masters [11]. For a three-layer network with n input neurons and m output neurons, the hidden layer would have $\sqrt{n \times m}$ neurons. The actual number of hidden neurons can still range from one-half to two times the geometric pyramid rule value depending on the complexity of the problem.

It is important to note that the rules which calculate the number of hidden neurons as a multiple of the number of input neurons implicitly assume that the training set is at least twice as large as the number of weights and preferably four or more times as large. If this is not the case, then these rules of thumb can quickly lead to overfitted models since the number of hidden neurons is directly dependent on the number of input neurons (which in turn determine the number of weights). The solution is to either increase the size of the training set or, if this is not possible, to set an upper limit on the number of input neurons so that the number of weights is at least half of the number of training facts. Selection of input variables becomes even more critical in such small networks since the luxury of the presenting the network with a large number of inputs and having it ignore the irrelevant ones has largely disappeared. Selecting the best number of hidden neurons involves experimentation. Three methods often used are the fixed, constructive and destructive. In the fixed approach, a group of neural networks with different numbers of hidden neurons are trained and each is evaluated on the testing set using a reasonable number of randomly selected starting weights. The increment in the number of hidden neurons may be one, two or more depending on the computational resources available. Plotting the evaluation criterion (e.g. sum of squared errors) on the testing set as a function of the number of hidden neurons for each neural network generally produces a bowl shaped error graph. The network with the least error found at the bottom of the bowl is selected because it is able to generalize best. This approach is time consuming, but generally works very well [11].

The constructive and destructive approaches involve changing the number of hidden neurons during training rather than creating separate networks each with a different number of hidden neurons, as in the fixed approach. Many commercial neural network software packages do not support the addition or removal of hidden neurons during training. The constructive approach involves adding hidden neurons until network performance starts deteriorating. The destructive approach is similar except that hidden neurons are removed during training.

Regardless of the method used to select the range of hidden neurons to be tested, the rule is to always select the network that performs best on the testing set with the least number of hidden neurons. When testing a range of hidden neurons it is important to keep all other parameters constant. Changing any parameter in effect creates a new neural network with a potentially different error surface which would needlessly complicate the selection of the optimum number of hidden neurons [11].

4.6.2 NUMBER OF OUTPUT NEURONS

Deciding on the number of output neurons is somewhat more straightforward since there are compelling reasons to always use only one output neuron. Neural networks with multiple outputs, especially if these outputs are widely spaced, will produce inferior results as compared to a network with a single output [11]. A neural network trains by choosing weights such that the average error over all output neurons is minimized.

Specialization also makes the trial and error design procedure somewhat simpler since each neural network is smaller and fewer parameters need to be changed to fine tune the final model [9].

4.6.3 TRANSFER FUNCTIONS

The majority of current neural network models use the sigmoid transfer function, but others such as the tangens hyperbolicus, arcus tangens and linear transfer functions have also been proposed [9].

Linear transfer functions are not useful for nonlinear mapping and classification. Transfer functions such as the sigmoid are commonly used for time series data because they are nonlinear and continuously differentiable which are desirable properties for network learning. Klimasauskas [7] states that if the network is to learn average behavior a sigmoid transfer function should be used while if learning involves deviations from the average, the tangens, hyperbolicus, function works best. In a standard backpropagation network, the input layer neurons typically use linear transfer functions while all other neurons use a sigmoid function.

4.7 EVALUATION OF THE SYSTEM

The most common error function minimized in neural networks is the sum of squared errors. Other error functions offered by software vendors include least absolute deviations, least fourth powers, asymmetric least squares and percentage differences. These error functions may not be the final evaluation criteria since other common forecasting evaluation methods such as the *mean absolute percentage error* (MAPE) are typically not minimized in neural networks.

4.8 TRAINING THE ANN

Training a neural network to learn patterns in the data involves iteratively presenting it with examples of the correct known answers. The objective of training is to find the set of weights between the neurons that determine the global minimum of the error function. Unless the model is overfitted, this set of weights should provide good generalization. The backpropagation network uses a gradient descent training algorithm which adjusts the weights to move down the steepest slope of the error surface. Finding the global minimum is not guaranteed since the error surface can include many local minima in which the algorithm can become"stuck". A momentum term" a partial dependence of the weight change at a certain learning step upon the weight change at the previous learning step" and five to ten random sets of starting weights can improve the chances of reaching a global minimum.

4.9 IMPLEMETATION

The implementation step is listed as the last one, but in fact requires careful consideration prior to collecting data. Data availability, evaluation criteria and training times are all shaped by the environment in which the neural network will be deployed. Most neural network software vendors provide the means by which trained networks can be implemented either in the neural network program itself or as an executable file. If not, a trained network can be easily created in a spreadsheet by knowing its architecture, transfer functions and weights. Care should be taken that all data transformations, scaling and other parameters remain the same from testing to actual use [9].

An advantage of neural networks is their ability to adapt to changing time series conditions through periodic retraining. Once deployed, a neural network's performance will degrade over time unless retraining takes place. However, even with periodic retraining, there is no guarantee that network performance can be maintained as the independent variables selected may have become less important.

It is recommended that the frequency of retraining for the deployed network should be the same as used during testing on the final model. However, when testing a large number of networks to obtain the final model, less frequent retraining is acceptable in order to keep training times reasonable. A good model should be robust with respect to retraining frequency and will usually improve as retraining takes place more often.

4.10 SUMMARY

This chapter presented the methods used to solve the time series prediction problems. Following, the design of neural network, were also presented.

CHAPTER 5

SIMULATION RESULTS

5.1 INTRODUCTION

In this chapter, three case studies, for various time series data, are considered.

5.2 CASE STUDY 1: SINUSOID PLUS SIMULATED GAUSSIAN WHITE NOISE

Example 1: In this example, 500 data points of this signal are used for training and evaluation. Signal frequency is 10 Hz, and the power of the signal is 1dB. Signal-to-noise ratio is 15 dB.

The prediction is based on seven past values $(x(t-1), x(t-2), x(t-3), x(t-4), x(t-5), x(t-6), x(t-7))$ and thus the output pattern is:

$$X(t) = f(x(t-1), x(t-2), x(t-3), x(t-4), x(t-5), x(t-6), x(t-7))$$

Data points were divided into three different sets: training set contains 393 data points, testing set contains 67 data points, and validation set contains 40 data points.

Chapter 5 *Simulation Results*

The polynomial neural network constructed is shown in Figure 5.1. The network contains three layers input, hidden, and output layer. Slab 1 represented input layer and contains 7 neurons with linear activation function.

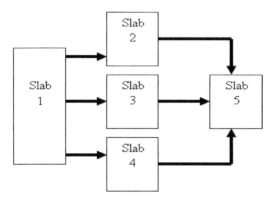

Figure 5.1: polynomial neural network.

Slab 2, 3, and 4 represented hidden layer and contains 9 neurons in each slab with Gaussian, Gaussian complement, and tanh (hyperbolic) activation functions, respectively. Slab 5 represented output layer and contains one neuron with logistic (sigmoid) activation function.

The results of the prediction can be seen in Figure 5.2 and Figure 5.3 respectively.

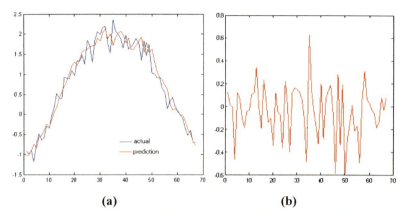

Figure 5.2: prediction of testing set: (a) prediction result and (b) prediction error.

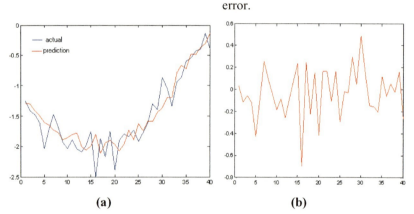

Figure 5.3: prediction of validation set: (a) prediction result and (b) prediction error.

Minimum average error in training set is 0.000012 and minimum average error in testing set is 0.000042 and validation set is 0.000031. The square of the correlation coefficient between actual and predicted output is 0.9215. Thus there is positive relationship between actual and predicted output.

Example 2: In this example, 500 data points of this signal are used for training and evaluation. Signal frequency is 15 Hz, and the power of the signal is 5dB. Signal-to-noise ratio is 10 dB.

The prediction is based on seven past values $(x(t-1), x(t-2), x(t-3), x(t-4), x(t-5), x(t-6), x(t-7))$ and thus the output pattern is:

$$X(t) = f(x(t-1), x(t-2), x(t-3), x(t-4), x(t-5), x(t-6), x(t-7))$$

Data points were divided into three different sets: training set contains 395 data points, testing set contains 66 data points, and validation set contains 39 data points.

The polynomial neural network constructed is shown in Figure 5.1. The results of the prediction can be seen in Figure 5.4 and Figure 5.5 respectively.

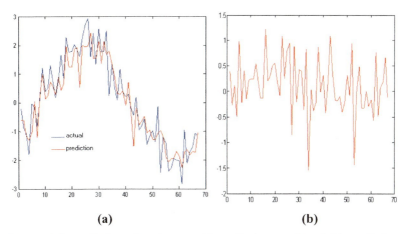

Figure 5.4: prediction of testing set: (a) prediction result and (b) prediction error.

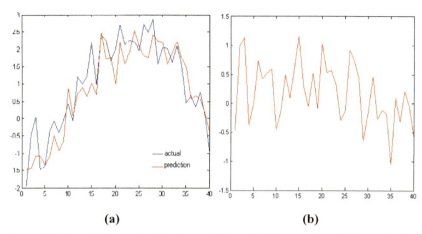

Figure 5.5: prediction of validation set: (a) prediction result and (b) prediction error

Minimum average error in training set is 0.000212 and minimum average error in testing set is 0.000072 and validation set is 0.0000065. The square of the correlation coefficient between actual and predicted output is 0.8854. Thus there is positive relationship between actual and predicted output.

Example 3: In this example, 500 data points of this signal are used for training and evaluation. Signal frequency is 20 Hz, and the power of the signal is 10 dB. Signal-to-noise ratio is 10 dB.

The prediction is based on seven past values $(x(t-1), x(t-2), x(t-3), x(t-4), x(t-5), x(t-6), x(t-7))$ and thus the output pattern is:

$$X(t) = f(x(t-1), x(t-2), x(t-3), x(t-4), x(t-5), x(t-6), x(t-7))$$

Data points were divided into three different sets: training set contains 397 data points, testing set contains 65 data points, and validation set contains 38 data points.

The polynomial neural network constructed is shown in Figure 5.1. The results of the prediction can be seen in Figure 5.6 and Figure 5.7.

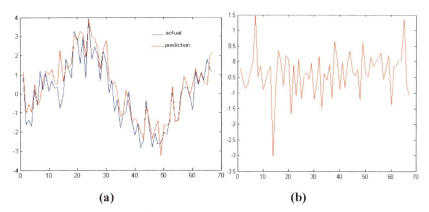

Figure 5.6: prediction of testing set: (a) prediction result and (b) prediction error.

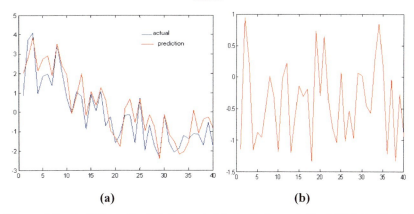

Figure 5.7: prediction of validation set: (a) prediction result and (b) prediction error

Minimum average error in training set is 0.000052 and minimum average error in testing set is 0.000032 and validation set is 0.000022. The square of the correlation coefficient between actual and predicted output is 0.9090. Thus there is positive relationship between actual and predicted output.

5.3 CASE STUDY 2: RIVER NILE BASIN

The Nile River Basin covers a large area of ~3 million km^2, approximately 10% of the African continent, and contains the longest river in the world, with a total length of approximately 6,700 km The basin is shared among 10 countries and extends from latitude 4° S to 31° N and from longitude 21° E to 40° E. Because of its size and variety of climates and topographies, it is one of the most complex major river basins in the world.

The Nile has three sources: the basin of the Equatorial Lakes plateau, the Ethiopian highland plateau, and the Bahr el Ghazal Basin. Almost 85% of the annual flow at Aswan in Egypt originates from precipitation on the Ethiopian Highlands through the Sobat, Blue Nile and Atbara Rivers. The remaining 15% originates from the Equatorial Lakes through the White Nile.

Rainfall in the Nile River Basin ranges from basically nil in most of Egypt and northern Sudan, to almost 2,100 mm on the Equatorial Lakes and the Ethiopian Highlands. The average total rainfall volume over the Nile River Basin is ~1,660,000 million mm^3. Less than 4% (55,500 mm^3) of this amount reaches Northern Africa through the Nile at the High Aswan Dam in Egypt, where it is fully utilized within the country before the river flows into the Mediterranean Sea. The average annual discharge of the Nile upstream of Egypt (84,000 mm^3) is less than 6% of the average total rainfall over the basin. The remaining 94% is kept upstream, where it is used, lost to groundwater seepage or evaporation, or stored in surface water bodies.

In this case, values of annual Nile flow from 1870 to 1970 are used for training and evaluation, [52]. The prediction is based on five past values $(x\ (t-1),\ x\ (t-2),\ x\ (t-3),\ x\ (t-4),\ x\ (t-5))$ and thus the output pattern is:

$$X\ (t) = f\ (x\ (t-1),\ x\ (t-2),\ x\ (t-3),\ x\ (t-4),\ x\ (t-5))$$

Data points are divided into three different sets: training set contains 63 data points, testing set contains 23 data points, and validation set contains 14 data points.

The polynomial neural network constructed is shown in Figure 5.8. The network contains three layers input, hidden, and output layer. Slab 1 represented input layer and contains 5 neurons with linear activation function.

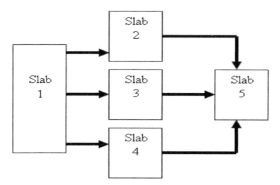

Figure 5.8: Network obtained for Nile flow

Slab 2, 3, and 4 represented hidden layer and contains 4 neurons in each slab with Gaussian, hyperbolic and Gaussian complement activation function, respectively. Slab 5 which represented output layer and contains one neuron with logistic activation function.

The results of the prediction can be seen in Figure 5.9 and Figure 5.10.

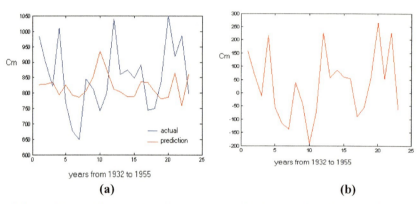

Figure 5.9: prediction of testing set: (a) prediction result and (b) prediction error.

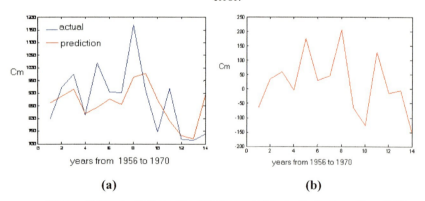

Figure 5.10: prediction of validation set: (a) prediction result and (b) prediction error.

Minimum average error in training set is 0.000024 and minimum average error in testing set is 0.000025 and validation set is 0.000035. The square of the correlation coefficient between actual and predicted output is 0.8420.

5.4 CASE STUDY 3: SUNSPOT

It was Galileo, in 1610, who made the first European observation of sunspot activity. Sunspots are relatively cooler areas on the Sun that are observed as dark patches. The number of sunspots observed indicates the amount of activity and the length of the solar cycle under observation. A great deal of research focuses on trying to predict sunspot activity. Scientists recommended combining the two best methods, which both use disturbances in the Earth's magnetic field as an indication of 'solar maxima', when the Sun is most active. Magnetic activity that accompanies the sunspots produces changes in the ultra-violet and soft x-ray emissions from the Sun with consequences for the Earth's upper atmosphere.

In this case, 255 data points of sunspot from 1700 to 1955 are used for training and evaluation, [53]. The prediction is based on four past values ($x(t-1)$, $x(t-2)$, $x(t-3)$, $x(t-4)$) and thus the output pattern is:

$$X(t) = f(x(t-1), x(t-2), x(t-3), x(t-4))$$

Data points were divided into three different sets: training set contains 165 data points, testing set contains 50 data points, and validation set contains 37 data points.

The polynomial neural network constructed is shown in Figure 5.11. The network contains three layers input, hidden, and output layer. Slab 1 represented input layer and contains 5 neurons with linear activation function.

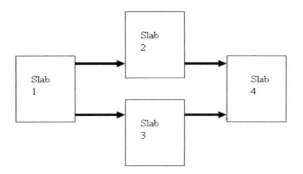

Figure 5.11 Network obtained for sunspot

Slab 2 and 3 represent the hidden layer and contains 4 neurons in each slab with Gaussian and Gaussian complement activation function, respectively.

Slab 4 represents the output layer and contains one neuron with logistic activation function.

The results of the prediction can be seen in Figure 5.12 and Figure 5.13.

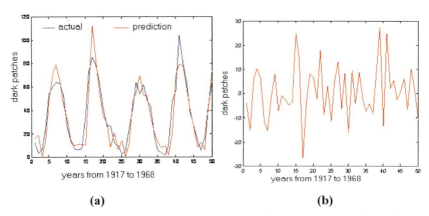

Figure 5.12: prediction of testing set: (a) prediction result and (b) prediction error.

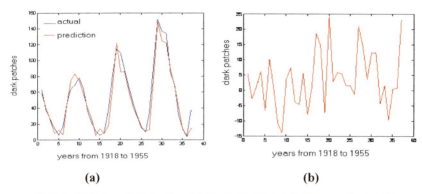

Figure 5.13: prediction of validation set: (a) prediction result and (b) prediction error.

Minimum average error in training set is 0.000072 and minimum average error in testing set is 0.000052 and validation set is 0.000041. The square of the correlation coefficient between actual and predicted output is 0.9333.

5.5 SUMMARY

This chapter presented simulation results of three examples of the Sinusoid plus simulated Gaussian white noise, the River Nile basin, and the Sunspot time series. Discussion for each case is also outlined.

CHAPTER 6

CONCLUSIONS AND FURTHER WORK

6.1 CONCLUSIONS

In the last decade, a large number of advanced methods of time-series prediction such as neural networks, genetic algorithms and other sophisticated computational methods have become popular. These different methods exhibit a certain degree of computational intelligence and perform better than others on specific problems. In forecasting systems such as neural networks, univariate predictions are based on previous observations and network architecture/ training algorithm must be optimized for accurate predictions. In statistical methods, the laws of prediction are more explicit and time-series must be analyzed first to identify the correct model for prediction.

This dissertation presented an overview of the work carried out for the project titled "*Time Series Prediction using Neural Networks*". The aim of this work is to explore the potential of the Artificial Neural Network in the field of time series prediction problems.

First, basic definitions of neural networks and time series signal were outlined. Also the various neural network architectures were studied. Models of neural networks and general learning rules were identified. Multi-layer feedforward and error back-propagation training algorithm were also investigated. Following, some other neural networks used in time series processing were presented.

Finally, steps of design artificial neural networks were investigated in details. Three time series were processed using neural networks. Results of the simulation, polynomial networks, prediction results, and actual prediction error were identified.

The quality and accuracy of the prediction relies on many factors. Neural networks can predict chaotic time series, the process of building being an elaborate process with a trial and error character. The results of the prediction can be refined furthermore by training the network, changing its parameters or changing the network type.

Main findings of the work can be summarized as follows:

1. Neural networks are a powerful tool for time series prediction, capable of outperforming most other known algorithms.

2. The potentially superior predictive power of neural networks can be exploited only if specific properties of the time series data are accounted for by means of appropriate pre- and postprocessing mechanisms.

3. Most promising directions of the research in the domain of neural networks in time series prediction are incorporation of textual data into prediction systems, statistical evaluation of neural network performance and

improving the comprehensibility of neural networks by symbolic rule extraction.

6.2 FURTHER WORK

The results obtained with the implemented method are very encouraging. In all problems tested there was a decrease in the prediction error.

One of the most important problems in the initial weights that started the training of network. Another problem is the suitable design of the neural network and activation function used to solve the problem.

An alternative approach would be to use a neural network with genetic algorithm as an evaluation computation. Approaches like that may obtain more advisable prediction results.

REFERENCES

[1] Hykin, Neural Network: A comprehensive Foundation, 2nd Edition, Prentice Hall, 1999.

[2] M. Minsky, S. Parpet , Perceptrons, MIT Press ,Cambridge , 1969.

[3] Cichocki A., Unbehauen R., Neural Networks For Optimization and Signal Processing, Weley, 1975.

[4] Jacek M. Zurada, Introduction to Artificial Network Systems, West Publishing Company, 2005.

[5] Ersoy, Tutorial at Hawaii International Conference on systems sciences, 1990.

[6] Ulbrich ,State Formation in Neural Networks for handling Temporal Information , PhD thesis, Institute fuer , Boston, 1991.

[7] C. C. Klimasauskas, Applying Neural Network, Probus, Chicago, 1993.

[8] D. P. Morgan, C. L. Scotfield, Neural Networks and speech processing , Kluwer Academic Publisher, 1991.

[9] Kaastra , M. Boyd, Designing a neural network for forecasting financial and economic time series , Neuro Computing, 1996.

References

[10] M. M. Nelson, W. T. Illingworth, A practical Guide to Neural Nets, Addison Wesley, 1991.

[11] Master, Practical Neural Network Recipes in C++, Academic Press, 1993.

[12] Hipel and Mcleod, 1994. URL http://www personal. buseco. monash. edu.au (URL accessed on June 5, 2008).

[13] Subba Rao and Gabr,1984. URL http://www-personal. buseco. monash. edu.au (URL accessed on June 5, 2008).

I want morebooks!

Buy your books fast and straightforward online - at one of the world's fastest growing online book stores! Environmentally sound due to Print-on-Demand technologies.

Buy your books online at
www.get-morebooks.com

Kaufen Sie Ihre Bücher schnell und unkompliziert online – auf einer der am schnellsten wachsenden Buchhandelsplattformen weltweit!
Dank Print-On-Demand umwelt- und ressourcenschonend produziert.

Bücher schneller online kaufen
www.morebooks.de

SIA OmniScriptum Publishing
Brivibas gatve 1 97
LV-103 9 Riga, Latvia
Telefax: +371 68620455

info@omniscriptum.com
www.omniscriptum.com

Druck:
Canon Deutschland Business Services GmbH
im Auftrag der KNV-Gruppe
Ferdinand-Jühlke-Str. 7
99095 Erfurt